JOSEPH PENNELL

1857–1926

JOSEPH PENNELL
ILLUSTRATOR, LITHOGRAPHER, ETCHER

Essay by Gėnė E. Harris

The Exhibition
January 11 through May 18, 1986

BRANDYWINE RIVER MUSEUM
Chadds Ford, Pennsylvania

This publication and the exhibition have been made possible by a grant from the Mabel Pew Myrin Trust.

FRONT COVER: Photograph of Joseph Pennell, 1922
   Courtesy of the Prints and Photographs Division,
   Library of Congress
FRONTISPIECE: 16 A FARM IN THE BROADS, 1895

The art of Joseph Pennell is a delightful discovery at any time. Among the host of American illustrators, there is a relatively small number whose work offers pleasure such as we immediately take in Pennell's drawings and prints. His talent was very fine, indeed; his sense of line and design are both wonderful. His commitment to illustration as important art was unwaivering and uncluttered by pejorative notions concerning commercial work.

It is long past time for a fresh and comprehensive look at Joseph Pennell's achievement, and it is appropriate that the Brandywine River Museum offer that opportunity. The Museum's rapidly growing collection of American illustration includes much work by Pennell and reveals diversity among his styles and subjects. In this publication and the exhibition it represents, Gėnė E. Harris, curator of collections, has assembled from many sources a wide variety of the artist's best work and commented extensively on his training and career. We know that her effort will bring pleasure to those who view the exhibition and we trust that it will help assure Joseph Pennell his deserved permanent, distinguished place in American art history.

James H. Duff
Director

ACKNOWLEDGEMENTS

For their assistance with research, I extend my sincere appreciation to Dr. Anne Cannon Palumbo, Benjamin Eisenstat, Robert F. Looney of the Free Library of Philadelphia, and Robert D. Schwarz of Frank S. Schwarz and Son.

I also wish to thank the generous lenders who helped make this exhibition a success: Childs Gallery, Boston and New York City; Mr. and Mrs. Benjamin Eisenstat; The Free Library of Philadelphia; Glenbow Museum, Calgary, Alberta; Illustration House, Inc.; The Library of Congress; The New York Public Library; The Philadelphia Museum of Art; Frank S. Schwarz and Son; and the Society of Illustrators, Museum of American Illustration.

This exhibition could not have been assembled without a much appreciated grant from the Mabel Pew Myrin Trust.

Gėnė E. Harris
Curator of Collections

40 A SKETCH, 1886

In the latter part of the nineteenth and early twentieth centuries, Joseph Pennell was one of America's leading illustrators. His pen line drawings, washes, etchings, and lithographs were among the first to present the aesthetic dimension of the urban industrial landscape. Inspired early in his career by European and American cultural and architectural monuments, he spent a lifetime creating numerous illustrations of streetscapes, cathedrals, palaces, and construction projects. For nearly fifty years his works enhanced the pages of two prominent publications, *Scribner's* and *Century*. His consuming interest in the aesthetics of the architectural environment won him considerable international fame, a fame far beyond what most artists would consider success. To top it all, throughout his career Pennell was a decided individualist not only in his art and writing but also in his life-style, which was marked by continual travels and numerous adventures. The history of the man and his personality are in large measure revealed in the course of his art.

Pennell was proud to be an illustrator, and from his childhood he surrendered everything to art. An only child, he began drawing at age four and illustrated his own imaginary stories. His first real subjects came from his neighborhood. The garden of his cousin's house faced Philadelphia's St. Peter's Church, and there, as a youth, he came to see the spires and to hear its chimes and bells: "these chimes," he later reminisced, "had much to do with making me . . . draw churches, 'steeple houses,' in which so much of my life, the best of my life, has been passed."[1]

The Pennells were a Quaker family whose ancestor Sir Robert Pennell came to Philadelphia in 1685. Other Pennells soon followed, all settling in the city. Joseph Pennell was born in a small row house on Ninth Street in Philadelphia on July 4, 1857. Four years later, his father, Larkin Pennell, a schoolteacher turned shipping supervisor, bought a larger home on nearby Lombard Street, a big three-story house with side and back yards. Here young Joseph grew up amid "perfect streets of . . . houses with white marble steps and green above."[2] His mother, Rebecca Barton Pennell, was an invalid, at least in her later years, and died in 1882 when Joseph, her only child, was twenty-five.

Of slight build, "Skinny Pennell," as the boys called him, preferred the company of girls since they engaged in less physical pastimes. He described himself as a "solitary little Quaker" and admitted, "I loved my drawing and my toys better than anything or anybody."[3] This passion for drawing was soon to trouble his parents. His father, a staunch Quaker conservative, wanted young Joseph to pursue studies in a field more practical than painting. Nevertheless, when Joseph remained unswerving, his father undertook to be his first teacher. Larkin Pennell

showed his only child how to grind colors and prepare materials for watercolors. Later, he paid for drawing and painting lessons. But despite this, he never endorsed Joseph's career.

A precocious child, Joseph was taught to read by his parents, who used among other books an illustrated *Aesop's Fables* and the *New England Primer*. The artist later claimed that these strenuous early lessons caused his vision to become impaired, a problem that plagued him all of his life. When his eyes did show some improvement, his parents enrolled him into the Friends Select Boys School in Germantown. The schoolrooms were stark, devoid of painting of any kind, for art was regarded as frivolous and distracting. Joseph sought a solitary place to practice his drawing and found it in his father's quiet office at Cope Brothers, where he could sit on a high stool and look out on the Delaware River. While perched on this stool by the window, Joseph drew the passing ships and supplemented them with ships that sailed into his imagination. Years later he remembered that the corner office gave him a special vantage point:

> I could look down Delaware Avenue on the Camden and Amboy Railroad Depot, and the Hotel with men always tilted back on chairs in a row in front of it; and the attempt to draw the street and the building and the people, as I saw them from above, gave me the mannerism, which I encourage, of looking down on subjects I draw to-day.[4]

In 1870, when Joseph was thirteen years old, the family moved to Fisher's Lane in Germantown, seven miles northwest of Philadelphia. Although the house did not particularly appeal to Joseph, he did enjoy the surrounding countryside. At the Friends school he was an indifferent student often hampered by insecurity. Looking back on these student days, Pennell described the six years spent at the school as being "awful . . . , the worst of [his] life."[5] The school did, however, institute one unusual innovation, a drawing class, and that interested him greatly.

William Henry Goodyear, who stressed architecture and taught with charts and diagrams, was Pennell's first art teacher and may be responsible for sparking Pennell's lifelong interest in architecture. After a short time, Goodyear was replaced by James Reid Lambdin, the former director of fine arts at the University of Pennsylvania. Pennell was intrigued by this newcomer. Lambdin encouraged students to look to nature as a teacher and yet to draw from memory: "to make you draw some object before you; then, not looking at it, to draw what you remembered of it." Next, Joseph Ropes—described by Pennell as "small, shy, modest,"—succeeded Lambdin as the drawing master. Ropes fueled Pennell's artistic

Photograph of Joseph Pennell at Adelphi Terrace
Courtesy of the Prints and Photographs Division, Library of Congress

ambitions by taking him on sketching excursions and by ensuring that Pennell received proper instruction in watercolor painting. But Ropes's approach was too academic for Pennell's informal tastes, and the young artist soon found the sessions too rigid and confining. At that point Pennell dropped out of the classes and turned to studying the work of magazine illustrators, sometimes even walking the seven miles to Philadelphia's Mercantile Library to study the drawings in *Scribner's Monthly, Harper's Weekly,* and *Harper's New Monthly.* His father brought home old copies of *Graphic, Art Journal, L'Art,* and *Portfolio* so that Joseph could copy sketches and even entered a subscription to *Scribner's* for his son. But Pennell later reminisced, "I . . . had to unlearn everything I picked up at that time. Had I been properly taught my craft, I would have been able to do far more and far better, for I have more brains than most people, but I had to unlearn everything and try to learn again in the right way later."[6]

In 1876, the year he was graduated from high school, Philadelphia hosted the International Centennial Exposition, at which some 7,000 paintings from twenty different countries were exhibited. Among the paintings displayed by artists from the United States were a number from Philadelphia, including works by Thomas Eakins, Christian Schussele, William Trost Richards, and Thomas Moran. Pennell eagerly attended the exposition throughout the summer and was inspired by the rich artistic display. Although excited by the works of the Europeans, he was especially impressed by American illustrators Edwin Austin Abbey and Charles Reinhart, "whom he observed sketching at the opening ceremonies from the gallery."[7]

After visiting the art gallery at the exposition, Pennell was determined to begin formal training in art and prepared a portfolio of sketches he had made from plaster casts. He submitted this to the examination committee of the Pennsylvania Academy of the Fine Arts. To his chagrin his application was rejected. He then submitted the same sketches to Harper and Brothers and once again they were rejected. Disillusioned, young Pennell decided that he was not meant to become an illustrator, so he took a job as a clerk in a coal company. His new career did not last long. About a year later the Philadelphia School of Industrial Art announced a series of evening classes to begin in the winter months of 1877 to 78. Pennell quickly submitted his portfolio, and he was accepted as a student.

Pennell's first instructor at the school, Charles M. Burns, Jr., was an architect who opposed all forms of copying and encouraged students to cultivate individual interpretations of their subjects. Teaching them to observe and to know their tools, Burns forced his students to work independently of their teacher. With this as a method, the class, more or less expelled from the studio, would often sketch

scenes across the city from "the Museum of Industrial Art to Cramp's Shipyard and the coal wharves in Kensington."[8] Under Burns, Pennell's drawings improved considerably, and he was determined to try again to become a student at the Pennsylvania Academy. Sympathetic to Pennell's ambitions, Burns persuaded the Academy to allow Pennell to enroll in a night class directed to the study of the classical form. The class was taught by Christian Schussele. Although it was during his tenure that life classes and dissection studies were introduced, Schussele's approach to painting was somewhat academic and conservative. Pennell soon tired of the regimen and decided to take instruction from Schussele's assistant Thomas Eakins. Eakins based his classes on the atelier system and emphasized drawing from nude models, intensive dissection studies, and the use of sculpture to understand form.

Under Eakins's tutelage, Pennell quickly advanced from formal studies of casts to life classes and began four years of instruction in oil painting with Eakins. Pennell still preferred working in pen and ink; however, Eakins had a strong influence on the development of Pennell's style. Decades later Pennell's art still revealed traces of Eakins's influence especially in his respect for past traditions and application of their lessons to the present. But, as is often the case between teachers and students, Eakins was critical of and sometimes disappointed in Pennell's choice of medium. Too sensitive, Pennell suffered under Eakins's criticism; his attendance at class grew more and more irregular and finally stopped. Nonetheless, during his four years at the Academy, Pennell had made lifelong friends among his fellow students including Thomas Anshutz, who later succeeded Eakins, Arthur Burdett Frost, Henry McCarter, J. J. Boyle, and Robert G. Leinroth, who, as art manager of Ketterlinus Lithographic Manufacturing Company, later collaborated with Pennell in producing many of his lithographs.

When Pennell set out to become an illustrator, conditions had never been more favorable. It was the dawn of the "Golden Age of Illustration," with Howard Pyle, Abbey, and Reinhart in the lead. Illustrators were in great demand. They were needed to satisfy an ever-growing public hunger for illustrated books, magazines, and newspapers. Etchers, engravers, and illustrators all shared the new popularity.

Late nineteenth-century Philadelphia was a center for the graphic arts, and even before Pennell left the Academy he had studied the works of artist-etchers such as John Sartain (1808–97) and Sartain's student Stephen Ferris (1835–1915). From Ferris, whom Pennell met in the 1870s, Pennell learned how to etch on copper in the traditional manner, and he came to share Ferris's admiration of Mariano Fortuny, a Spanish draftsman whose works were exhibited in America

Photograph of Joseph Pennell in the process of etching, circa 1920
Courtesy of the Prints and Photographs Division, Library of Congress

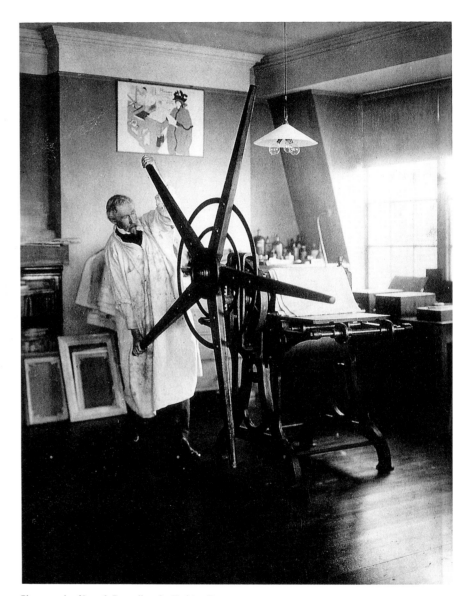

Photograph of Joseph Pennell at the Etching Press
Courtesy of the Prints and Photographs Division, Library of Congress

and whose etchings were widely sold. After studying Fortuny's work in detail a bit later in his career, Pennell produced architectural landscapes with a similar dashing and atmospheric fluid line. Fortuny's drawings, however, were just one influence in the development of Pennell's smooth, easy style; English illustrators also shaped his approach.

Shortly after he had enrolled in the School of Industrial Art, Pennell had received his first commission as an illustrator. This came as a result of his studies of old prints in the library of the Historical Society of Pennsylvania. In spring 1878, Pennell had composed some drawings based upon some old prints of historic Germantown. Frederick D. Stone, a neighbor on Fisher's Lane, saw the drawings and introduced Pennell to Townsend Ward, a writer who was preparing a series of articles on Philadelphia's historical places for the historical society's *Pennsylvania Magazine of History and Biography*. Pleased by the young artist's skill, Ward asked him to illustrate the articles. Pennell prepared a series of etchings, suggestively European in style, of local historical buildings in and around Germantown, including *Old Rising Sun Inn* (cat. 29), *Fox Chase Inn* (cat. 16), *Stenton, from the Southwest* (cat. 41), and *Wakefield Mills* (cat. 51). These carefully composed etchings convey a pleasant feeling of familiarity. Through a subtle manipulation of line, Pennell created a whole range of black tones that describes the surface, the structure, and the texture of the buildings. These etchings have the characteristics of a tightly woven tapestry. Combinations of Pennell's architectural etchings and drawings ran as a series in the society's journal between 1879 and 1881; later the whole series reappeared, with the addition of three etchings by Blanche Dillaye, in a limited-edition portfolio, "Views on the Old Germantown Road."

During the 1870s as interest in etching increased, clubs were formed: the New York Etching Club was established in 1877, and the Philadelphia Society of Etchers was founded in 1880. The first active members of the latter group were Ferris and Peter Moran. Still a student at the Academy, Pennell asked to join and became an enthusiastic member. The society provided him with an unparalleled opportunity to exchange his ideas with other artist-etchers. And, as a club member, he was able to examine and study the works of one of the country's most prolific collectors of engravings and etchings, James L. Claghorn.

Pennell's growing interest in etching also led him to study the works of James McNeill Whistler, who produced his first set of etchings in Paris in 1858. Soon after joining the society, Pennell began a series of etchings of Philadelphia that clearly evidence Whistler's influence. As art historian Anne Palumbo has pointed out, *Callowhill Street Bridge* (1880) and *Sauerkraut Row* (1881) "are markedly similar to" Whistler's *Black Lion Wharf* (1859) and *The 'Adam' and 'Eve,' Old Chelsea* (1879), "especially in their flat, horizontal formats, the careful, detailed treatment

accorded the old houses, and the emphasis on surface textures and varying rooflines."[9] At the same time, Pennell's own style was developing and improving; indeed, while composing this series, he became absorbed in the study of etching and carefully experimented with various methods of preparing the copperplates.

Pen-and-ink illustration also continued to claim his attention as the 1880s began, and Pennell again approached both Scribner's and Harper's for commissions. Scribner's was the first to commission him. An article in *Scribner's* on lower Manhattan's Shanty Town had given Pennell the idea of preparing a series of sketches of an area along the Delaware River near Philadelphia known as "the Ma'sh." These were unlike the etchings that he had earlier composed for the Historical Society of Pennsylvania in both subject matter and, especially, technique. For this set of images, he used heavy accents and broad hatchings to break the surfaces into geometric designs and thereby create livelier and more direct images.

The success with Scribner's fixed Pennell onto a career as an illustrator. He established his studio at 1334 Chestnut Street, sharing it with a fellow artist, Harry Poore; his neighbors were artists Cecilia Beaux and Stephen and Maxfield Parrish. Hardly settled in the building, he received a commission from Century Company, which was publishing *Scribner's Monthly* under the new name *Century Magazine*, to illustrate an article on the Dunker settlement at Ephrata, Pennsylvania. In preparation, Pennell traveled to Ephrata to make preliminary sketches and took Poore to help in drawing figures. Nearly fifty years later, Pennell described the assignment:

> On the hill at Ephrata stood, and still stand—though one is gone, fallen down through neglect and decay—the monastic houses, copies of South German buildings with huge high roofs; and within are the cells of the brothers and sisters, the Meeting House and the work-rooms. We went at the drawings with fury, but, to our horror, we found that Howard Pyle had been there, for he had left behind an unfinished drawing which was preserved in the hotel. We said nothing, but worked harder and faster, fearing that any month Pyle's article might appear in *Harper's* and ours never be printed. . . . My work was finished on the spot, all done from nature. This is the right way to illustrate. I have always worked this way when possible and not copied sketches. . . . Pyle's drawings only appeared years after, and, though we trembled every month when *Harper's* was announced, we came out in *The Century* years before he did in *Harper's*.

One pencil-and-wash drawing that Pennell executed on location, *The Brothers' and Sisters' Houses* (cat. 11), was subsequently engraved on wood for an article, "A

2 AN AFTERNOON CALL, 1889

18 HOVETON CHURCH, 1895

4 APPROACH TO NORWICH, 1895

Colonial Monastery." Drawn with less sharply defined details than Pennell had used before, it reveals a more painterly sense of the play of light and shadow, giving it a soft image, an almost sooty quality.[10]

A. W. Drake, then the art editor at *Scribner's* and *Century*, praised Pennell's drawings of Ephrata and gave him a similar assignment to nearby Bethlehem's Moravian settlement. Pennell, pleased, wrote his father in May 1881:

> And more luck, . . . Drake likes the Bethlehem things very much, and
> wants me to make a drawing of an old house outside of Boston, so I shant
> be home before 4th day—and he is going with me to Virginia and we wont
> go till about the 3d week of June, so I can do something for Stone.[11]

To encourage their promising young illustrator, when Drake accompanied Pennell to Virginia he brought a list of subjects that might be illustrated. They went to Antietam where Pennell made drawings for the Battles and Leaders of the Civil War series and then to Washington, D.C., to illustrate an article on the Corcoran Gallery of Art.

That same May, Drake had asked, "Will you please send me, say—eight of your *very best* etchings of old Historical Buildings about Philadelphia with notes of description." The etchings that Pennell chose for this assignment were much larger in scale than he used for the Ma'sh. They ranged from picturesque depictions of Philadelphia's riverfront to crowded streets and historic inns. R.W. Gilder, who soon succeeded Drake as art editor of *Century*, was pleased with the etchings and sent Philadelphia-born Elizabeth Robins, the intended writer of the accompanying article, to Pennell's studio. A three-year courtship followed and a lifelong series of collaborations resulted from this meeting of artist and author. Years later Elizabeth described their meeting:

> After all these years, I still wonder which amazed me most, the artist or the
> studio. . . . What I found was a large bare room, a dusty floor without car-
> pet, a high ceiling, a large uncurtained window. . . . Nothing was on the
> two easels, a few drawings were pinned on the wall. . . . The artist waiting
> for us was young, tall, exceedingly thin, with brown hair, brown mous-
> tache and shortish brown beard, deep-set grey-green eyes, intent and seri-
> ous beyond his years, holding one's attention at once. I remember thinking
> him a strange combination of shyness and self-possession.[12]

Although admittedly shy, Pennell talked confidently of his illustrations for the article; where his art was concerned, he was wholly self-reliant. Artist and author soon began work on their project, starting with walks through the city. Pennell's enthusiasm for the city was contagious, and he helped Elizabeth to see Philadelphia as he did, with a clear focus on its architectural features. They spent many hours exploring the city, finding picturesque places that he could draw and she could write about. By the end of the year, their work on the article was completed, so together they sought a new project. At about the same time, a new journal, *Our Continent*, was launched in Philadelphia, and Pennell was one of the illustrators commissioned to execute some drawings. Pennell, in turn, suggested Elizabeth as a possible collaborator, and together they produced a piece on Philadelphia's shops and old churches. This type of collaboration eventually became a lifetime pattern.

While the two were looking for joint commissions, Century eagerly offered Pennell to illustrate William Dean Howells's articles on Tuscany. The commission came in May 1882, but the artist turned suitor postponed leaving for Europe until the following January, even though he would receive $600 for six months work. In the interim, Pennell contributed to an exhibition of the Philadelphia Society of Etchers that opened December 27, 1882, and which included works by almost every noteworthy American etcher—including Thomas and Mary Moran, Charles Platt, John Twachtman, Theodore Wendel—and several European etchers—notably Camille Corot, Charles Daubigny, and Mariano Fortuny. Pennell helped to plan and assemble the exhibition but decided to exhibit simply his etchings from his own personal collection. He also worked on a display that compared the etching process of wood engraving and that of photoengraving, one that revolutionized the art of illustration.

Finally in January 1883, he joined the Howellses in Florence. Although somewhat reserved at their first meeting, the three soon became closely acquainted. Pennell accompanied the Howellses as they traveled about Tuscany and made sketches and etchings of scenes in Siena, Lucca, and Fiesole, among others. William Dean Howells had previously written the popular *Venetian Days* (1867) and *Italian Journeys* (1886), and a grand project had been planned to write semihistorical essays on thirteen Tuscan cities. The pressures of his other work prevented his doing this project, and instead he decided to write only about Florence and a few towns within an easy traveling distance. In a letter to Elizabeth, Pennell described their adventures:

> I have been running around with Howells—yesterday we started from
> [Pisa]—and drove across the country to Lucca. I am getting along very
> much better with him than I did at first—and if he wasent [sic] going to
> Venice next week—I would probably fall desperately in love with him—as I
> did with [author George W.] Cable—But that ride over the flat Compagna,
> with Pisa silhouetted behind us, up into the narrow passes and through
> jolly old towns each one of which I could spend a lifetime in—but we didn't
> stop—Still this the way to see Italy.[13]

22 INTERIOR OF YORK MINSTER, circa 1880
Courtesy of Childs Gallery, Boston and New York City

Working with an exuberantly free and energetic line, Pennell prepared several delicate etchings, including *The Ponte Vecchio, Florence* (cat. 33) and *The Swing of the Arno, Pisa* (cat. 46). For an artist who was already skilled in depicting architectural subjects, the richness and variety he found in Tuscany provided Pennell with all the material he craved: "the country is overpowering—everything is worth doing and you can't touch it." Italy's indescribable beauty added a grace to Pennell's etchings and intensified his rich treatment of the terrain and his inimitable accentuation of buildings, bridges, water, and vistas. His etchings show a mature style and convey an unmistakable vitality. They also demonstrate that Pennell's architectural draftsmanship was far more developed than his skill in anatomy; although he had studied the nude under Eakins, he had not mastered the human body, and the few figures that usually appear in these landscapes are "stiffly posed, and seldom integrated into the scene."[14]

While in Florence, in between the trips to nearby cities, Pennell enjoyed the company of many colleagues, especially artist Frank Duveneck (1848–1919). Duveneck had just arrived from Munich, and Pennell, joining Duveneck and his cohorts, spent many evenings in the local trattoria heatedly discussing art. Pennell was particularly interested in Duveneck's etchings, and together the two found time to print their etchings and compare techniques. Pennell also visited Venice, which was an especially appealing and picturesque city for etchers at the time. In fact, Pennell's light and free-flowing etchings of the water-bound city, which appeared in *Century* and other popular publications, contributed to the tourists' rediscovery of the city.

In late autumn 1883, his work for Howells completed, Pennell returned to America. In January, he became engaged to Elizabeth, and they married five months later. Elizabeth's career had developed rapidly. Her essays were being published in *The Atlantic Monthly* and *Century*. Pennell encouraged his wife's literary ambitions, and they agreed that they would continue their own careers after marriage, combining efforts where feasible. They decided to honeymoon in Italy so that they could write and illustrate a story on tricycling from Florence to Rome for *Century*. A cholera epidemic in Italy changed their plans, so they sailed to England instead. Once there, they journeyed to Canterbury so that Joseph could complete a portfolio. Elizabeth wrote an amusing narrative about the trip. The story, *Canterbury Pilgrimage* (1885), was published by Charles Scribner's Sons, and it marked the first of the Pennells' many joint travel books written during their thirty years abroad. In just five years following their marriage, they collaborated on four additional travel books, *An Italian Pilgrimage* (1887), *Our Sentimental Journey through France and Italy* (1888), *Two Pilgrims' Progress from Fair Florence to Eternal Rome* (1887–89), and *Our Journey to the Hebrides* (1889). On the whole,

these and their other travel books were generally light and pleasantly informative, and they emphasized the excitement of travel.

Late in the fall of 1884, the Pennells were finally able to take their long-delayed Italian honeymoon and completed "Italy from a Tricycle." They arrived in Rome during the festival season and remained for several months. During their stay, Pennell produced a number of well-executed pen-and-ink figure drawings. Unlike figures in his earlier works, these are animated and drawn in a variety of casual poses. *Noontime* (cat. 27), for example, is typical of his figural compositions showing a friendly gathering of peasants for a noon repast. Emphatically linear, the figures are rendered with sharply defined lines, and the use of light and shade gives amplitude to their forms. The drawings are confidently drawn; nonetheless, they reveal the artist's continued inability to grasp the vital character of anatomy. It is understandable that the editors at Century Company preferred Pennell's architectural drawings to his figural compositions.

In the spring of 1885 as the Pennells reluctantly left Italy "blossoms were showing above high garden walls, and market carts were laden with fresh fruit and vegetables." They returned to their Bloomsbury lodgings in London and began a major commission on English cathedrals for Century. At first unenthusiastic, Pennell soon warmed to the beauty of these buildings and took delight in those he visited. Their impact grew upon him with every drawing he made. Although not published until 1890, *The English Cathedrals* proved to be a learning experience "not so much in archeological and architectural forms nor principle of construction, but rather in pictorial composition." The beauty that he found in the Salisbury Cathedral enabled him to understand impressionist art, and this, in time, helped him to define his own aesthetic:

> I hunted and hunted for his points of view, which give all the dignity and beauty of the place—for these cathedral closes are beautiful—and all the feeling of it, but I never could find the spots he had found. And then, for the first time, it began to dawn on me, dimly, vaguely, that what I must do was what has been done by every great artist who has made compositions; though compositions that give the effect often are not true, I learned. I found out, too, that I must also give the feeling of the place, really the feeling, the impression, it made on me. This is impressionism and not the putting down of spots, blots, cubes, or other mannerisms. This is the impressionism of Piero della Francesca, Velasquez, Claude, Turner, Constable, Whistler. It is not rendering the subject as it is, but giving the sensation it makes on you, and if that sensation is strong enough, others will feel it. That is impressionism—art.[15]

34 PORTRAIT OF WASHINGTON LAKER
FROM A PHOTOGRAPH BY ULKE, n.d.

21 IN A LOCK, circa 1889
   Courtesy of the Print Division,
   The New York Public Library, Astor,
   Lenox and Tilden Foundations

38 A RIVER TRAIN OR TOWED DOWN, 1886

In 1886, while working on the cathedral project, Pennell received a sudden and short cable from the art editors at Century: "Postpone the Cathedral for the Plantin Museum [in Antwerp] which is wanted at once." At the very same time, author Philip Gilbert Hamerton wrote, "Join me in my boat down the Saône from its source to Lyons, to do an illustrated book." Pennell decided that the cathedrals and Hamerton had to wait. He immediately packed his bags and sailed to Antwerp to draw *Interior, Plantin Museum, Antwerp* (cat. 23) and *Street in Antwerp with Plantin House* (cat. 43). Although he found both the exterior and the interior of the museum building "wonderfully fine" and "stunning," he was less than enthusiastic about the collection which he described as rooms filled with "sprawling Rubenses—each one worse than the other."[16] Pennell's pen-and-ink drawings of the museum and its environs are executed with fluidity; the cross-hatchings and the sumptuous detail combine to convey the medieval beauty of the place. The resulting images are once again similar to the work of Mariano Fortuny.

While finishing work on the Plantin Museum, Pennell received another pleading letter from Hamerton, again urging him to make a trip on the Saône. Pennell, eager to leave Antwerp, arranged to meet on Hamerton's large French canal boat, the *Boussemroum*, in the town of Gray on the Haute Saône. As soon as the journey commenced, the two men's cordial relationship began to deteriorate. It became for both Hamerton and Pennell a rancorous journey in hot and cramped quarters. The two men parted less than friends. In 1925, Pennell wrote his version of the journey which appeared in the *New York Times Magazine* and in his autobiography, *The Adventures of an Illustrator*. Despite his difficulties during the river voyage and his wife's later pronouncement that Hamerton's book was "dull," Pennell composed some of his most beautiful and delicate sketches on that trip. *A Sketch* (cat. 40), *The Bridge at Chemilly* (cat. 7), *Ovanches—The Cross* (cat. 30), *The Towers of Tournus* (cat. 48), *The Quay at Trevoux* (cat. 35), and *Ile Barbe from the East* (cat. 19) reveal picturesque tiny villages struggling up hillsides, an enchanting countryside that Pennell himself called "really lovely and simple." There is a careless ease with which the trees are sketched and the atmosphere is conveyed by the soft pen strokes. Some distant views show a precise landscape, confined to a small band stretching across the middle of an otherwise empty page. These sketches, some of the best work of his life, are more suggestive than are his more complex landscapes. Like most of his works, these drawings were created directly from nature and impart a very personal feeling of the place. Pennell, however, confessed to Elizabeth:

> I really am awfully lonely, not at all satisfied with what I have done—and anxious to get at the Cathedrals again. Either Hamerton is or we are utterly wrong in our ways of making books—but I think it utterly senseless to go on spinning out a book—when it is already full and complete—just to make something long out of it—and to do the whole river.[17]

Upon his return to England Pennell completed large architectural drawings of Westminister Abbey and a London series entitled "From Charing Cross to St. Paul's" for *Century*, and he illustrated Henry James's articles on London, also for *Century*. Yet, with all of these commissions, Pennell managed to squeeze in a trip to Switzerland's Matterhorn and Zermatt region to compose illustrations for an article on the Alps. To give authenticity to his drawings, he—accompanied by guides and carrying ropes and axes—climbed one of the difficult horns to make a sketch. This trip provided to be costly; he made sketches on a subject wholly new to him, and the completed drawings were not to his liking. Only one of the more attractive sketches that he created, *An Off Day at Zermatt* (cat. 3), was reproduced, with his article "Play and Work in the Alps," in *Century* (1891).

For several years the Pennells had lived a nomadic life on various assignments. But in 1891, tiring of travel, they finally decided to settle in London in Adelphi, a section rich in literary associations. Their neighbors included authors John Galsworthy and George Bernard Shaw. Among their frequent visitors were painter-illustrator Walter Crane and James McNeill Whistler, the latter of whom years before had influenced Pennell's work. Most of Whistler's lithographs dated back to the 1870s, but during the long illness of his wife in the 1890s he again turned to lithography. Pennell made frequent visits to Whistler's home and watched the great artist at work painting the portraits of famous men and scenes of Paris and London as well as making lithographs. It is not surprising that Pennell's lithographs and etchings of New York, London, and Philadelphia made during this period have the style and directness of Whistler's work. Like Whistler, Pennell drew his subject directly on a copperplate, initially using what was known as the Whistler needle. In later prints, he used a dental tool which he had reshaped for his purpose. Frederick Keppell, one of his dealers, recalled how Pennell worked:

> He chooses his place in the crowded street and stands there quite undisturbed by the rush of passers—or by the idlers who stand and stare at him or his work. Taking quick glances at the scene he is depicting, he rapidly draws his line with the etching needle upon the copperplate which he holds in his other hand. The print which eventually resulted was the reverse of the actual scene—like a mirror image.[18]

19 ILE BARBE FROM THE EAST, 1886

A more pleasant commission that came Pennell's way during the 1890s was to illustrate Anna Bowman Dodd's "Cruise on the Norfolk Broads." The commission was very tempting, giving Pennell the chance to get away from the hectic London life and once again enjoy the tranquility of the countryside. He found the simplicity of Norfolk charming. In addition to a number of pen-and-ink drawings, he composed a series of monochrome washes. *Hoveton Church* (cat. 18) and *A Farm in the Broads* (cat. 15), especially, are dreamy landscapes composed with delicate brush strokes that convey a subtle romantic character: "the low, flat stretches of meadowland and water, the boats that in the distance seemed sailing and drifting through the fields, the ghostly effects in the morning mist, the local regattas, the secluded villages, the old-fashioned towns—Yarmouth, Norwich."[19] The illustrated article was immediately published in *Century* in 1895, and the following year the illustrations appeared in Dodd's book *The Broads*, published by Macmillan and Company.

By 1899, Pennell had distinguished himself as a travel author. Because of his popular series on England's highways and byways, Macmillan asked him to compose illustrations for a similar guidebook, *Highways and Byways of Normandy*, to be written by the Reverend Percy Dearmer. Pennell traveled to France and created a number of illustrations—*Abbaye Aux Hommes, Caen* (cat. 1), *St. Sauveur, Caen* (cat. 44), and *Tower, Church of St. Jacques, Dieppe* (cat. 47)—all of which convey the picturesqueness of the romantic French landscape. This recalled an earlier visit with his bride, and he wrote to Elizabeth that "his love of the beauty of 'the French scene' had not lost its ardour."[20]

Early in 1904, Pennell decided to return to America, having lived abroad for twenty years. His desire to return to his native land was in large measure based on his never fully surrendering himself to the Old World. Although he loved England, and especially London, "he remained an adamant even bumptious Yankee, assuring English friends of the glories of 'God's Country' and joining delightedly with Whistler in frequent digs at the 'Islanders.'" Whistler's death in 1903 certainly quickened Pennell's decision to leave London. Perhaps he also remembered his last visit to America in 1893 to view the World's Columbian Exposition and how intrigued he was by the rapid changes that had taken place there, particularly in architecture. "The buildings are simply perfect," he wrote "it's like an old master—a Claude from the National Gallery up to date."[21]

Arriving in New York in late 1904, Pennell decided that the city embodied all the dynamism of the new century. Captivated by the hectic building activity and the rising structures, he quickly produced over sixty etchings and lithographs. "It's so beautiful," he enthused, "I must go out and make more immortal masterpieces—the mill is grinding and when it is I don't like to stop."[22] Such etchings as *The Cliffs, The Statue of Liberty, Canyon No. 1*, and *The Times Building* depict landscapes of majestic skyscrapers rising sharply upward like mountains. These images harken back to his early drawings of the cathedrals and monumental buildings on the European landscape.

Extremely prolific during this period, Pennell executed a number of his most poignant and dramatic works. He began experimenting with new tonal media, producing in 1908 quality mezzotints of New York and London. *From Cortland Street Ferry, Hail America*, and *Flatiron Building* not only reveal Whistlerian touches of abstract shapes and exploitation of night effects but also show Pennell's own innovative printing techniques. These allowed him to obtain a variety of effects. Pennell skillfully "circumvented the laborious task of working over the plate with a rocker by roughening the plate with sandpaper in the press." The sandpaper technique enabled him to achieve pale grays in *Flatiron Building* and bold blackness in *From Cortland Street Ferry*. Pennell summed up his printing experiences with these remarks:

> Printing may be a sore trial to patience and temper so are most things—but when you do get a good print you have something—and in Editions of the size I do I don't get tired—except physically—for it is hard work—of course Goulding [the printer Frederick Goulding] can follow a model you set him perfectly—but then the charm of etching-printing is that you don't follow a model—when you do it yourself—you have an idea of what you want and may-be you get that—but as soon as you have got it—you see something else and go for that and with a result, as I am perfectly aware, that when I have done 25 I am just about where I would like to have started, I have just about got the press, and the ink, and the paper right—and got them to work together—it is all to me a series of experiments—which sometimes never come right—sometimes though, the plate comes right with the second proof—sometimes but rarely the first is the best you can do. But all the same it is amusing—and I like it—and so long as I can manage it, no one else shall print my plates.[23]

Perhaps his most beautiful studies of the emerging skyscraper were those of the Woolworth Building in 1915. It was then the tallest building in New York City. Pennell had watched it grow from ground-breaking in 1912 to its completion three years later. It can be likened to a cathedral tower rising majestically over the city.

During the 1905–15 era, Pennell was acclaimed as the premier artist of the skyscraper, and his compelling images were reproduced not only in *Century* but also in various other magazines and books, among them John C. Van Dyke's *New New York* (1908). The beauty of the architectural landscape so well captured

14 THE CUT LOOKING TOWARD CALEBRA, circa 1912
   Courtesy of Frank S. Schwarz and Son

by Pennell compared favorably with the best of European masterpieces. At least one critic hailed Pennell as the "discoverer one might almost say the inventor of the skyscraper beautiful."[24]

Given his many commissions, it comes as a surprise to discover that 1912 was the most active year of Pennell's working life. It was a one of almost uninterrupted travel and work. In late 1911, while on a commission in Rome, he convinced the art editors at Century to assign him a project in Panama and traveled from Rome to Panama via New York. The Panama commission was an important assignment. He wanted to create a series of drawings and lithographs depicting the building of the Panama Canal. When he arrived, he settled to working immediately, and his method of working astonished many. "He sauntered along, portfolio and campstool under his arm, his waistcoat pockets full of pencils, his eyes half shut in the artist's way which suggests sleepiness to the uninitiated. 'Don't look like much!' the man who worked the steam shovel said, when told that this was an artist of distinction."[25] Later, after seeing some of Pennell's sketches, the workman changed his opinion, and at the end of the visit Pennell presented him with a lithograph.

The massive canal project had captured the attention of the whole world. For Pennell, Panama proved to be all that he had hoped for. The building of the canal was just at the stage where he would have found it the most captivating. His depictions of the grand endeavor, with its mighty locks and earth-moving equipment. are an impressive record of the greatest engineering achievements of the age: *The Cut Looking toward Ancon Hill* (cat. 13), *The Gates of Pedro Miguel* (cat. 17), *The Cranes at Miraflores Lock* (cat. 12), and *The Cut Looking toward Calebra* (cat. 14). One of the most famous of Pennell's lithographs was *Laying the Floor of Pedro Miguel Lock*, and Pennell vividly recalled the scene:

> Here I went to the bottom and looked up between the huge walls outside the gates, spanned with arches and buttresses—one of the most stupendous, most decorative compositions I have ever seen. When I asked the engineer—Mr. Williamson—how he had come to make the splendid springing lines of his arches and buttresses, he said it was only done to save concrete.[26]

In Panama, Pennell struggled to capture graphically what he called the "Wonder of Work." His images are of huge cranes, massive locks, powerful engines, all set against a steaming army of indistinguishable workmen. The Panama lithographs first appeared in *Century Magazine*, without text. Shortly afterward they were published in the *New York Times* with Pennell's notes as a special Sunday supplement that sold out immediately. The twenty-eight lithographs also enjoyed considerable popularity in England and Italy and were subjects of special exhibitions at London's Fine Arts Society and Florence's Sala Leonardo da Vinci.[27] Copies were highly acclaimed and purchased by many institutions—including the Library of Congress, Pennsylvania Academy of the Fine Arts, Brooklyn Museum, Victoria and Albert Museum, and Uffizi Gallery—and by countless individuals.

After completing the Panama lithographs, Pennell received a silver medal from the Royal Society of Arts. In his acceptance address to the society, he drew grand parallels between his own interest in huge architectural forms and Rembrandt's fascination with his father's mill, Claude's interest in harbors and lighthouses, Canaletto's interest in Venetian building, and Piranesi's interest in Carceri (fantastic imaginary prisons) and added:

> Work today is the greatest thing in the world, and the artist who records it will be best remembered. . . . I went to Panama because I believed that, in the making of the greatest work of modern times, I should find my greatest inspiration. . . . So I started on a trip of 15,000 miles in search of the most Wonderful of Work in the world.[28]

Pennell's life ended in much the way it had begun, with a seemingly unquenchable desire to work as an artist. But at sixty-nine years of age his vitality and his unrivaled energy were exhausted. He died of pneumonia on April 23, 1926, and was buried in the Friends' cemetery in Germantown. John Copley's homage to his colleague and friend best describes Pennell's legacy: "Pennell has done great notable things. He has triumphed over the difficulties and produced a magnificent output of prints full of every quality that it should posses; he is a great artist and a great leader in all forms of black and white art."[29]

Pennell's distinguished career lasted some fifty years. As a famous illustrator-printmaker he contributed hundreds of drawings for books and magazines. As an author his writings on the subject of graphic arts exerted a strong influence on both European and American artists. He was not the first American illustrator either in time or in talent, nor is he the last; however, he will always be among the best and most representative of illustrators.

30 OVANCHES—THE CROSS, 1886

53 Untitled Illustration, circa 1888
Courtesy of Mr. and Mrs. Benjamin Eisenstat

CATALOGUE OF THE EXHIBITION

1 ABBAYE AUX HOMMES, CAEN, circa 1904
Pen and ink on paper, 11 × 15½ inches
Lent by the Print Division, The New York Public Library,
Astor, Lenox, and Tilden Foundations
Illustration for Percy Dearmer's *Highways and Byways in
Normandy.* London: Macmillan and Company, 1904.

2 AN AFTERNOON CALL, 1889
Wash on paper glued to board, 8¾ × 11¹/₁₆ inches
Brandywine River Museum. The Jane Collette Wilcox
Collection
Illustration for Joseph and Elizabeth Robins Pennell's *The
Stream of Pleasure.* London: Macmillan and Company,
1891.

3 AN OFF DAY AT ZERMATT, 1891
Pen and ink on paper, 6¾ × 8 inches
Collection of the Glenbow Museum, Calgary, Alberta
Illustration for Joseph Pennell's "Play and Work in the
Alps," *The Century Magazine,* June 1891.

4 APPROACH TO NORWICH, 1895
Wash on illustration board, 12¹/₁₆ × 18 inches
Brandywine River Museum. The Jane Collette Wilcox
Collection
Illustration for Anna Bowman Dodd's *On the Broads.*
London: Macmillan and Company, 1896.

5 AT THE FOOT OF THE CROSS, 1884
Pen and ink on paper, 15¼ × 11³/₈ inches
Collection of Glenbow Museum, Calgary, Alberta
Illustration for Joseph and Elizabeth Pennell's *Two
Pilgrims' Progress From Fair Florence to Eternal City of
Rome.* Boston: Roberts Brothers, 1886. Also illustrated in
the Pennells' *An Italian Pilgrimage.* London: Seeley and
Company, 1887, 1889.

6 BELOW THE CHESTNUT STREET BRIDGE, 1884
Etching, 18⁷/₈ × 15 inches
Collection of the Brandywine River Museum
Published in the New York Etching Club's *Twenty Origi-
nal Etchings.* New York: Cassell and Company, 1884.

SAAL UND SARON.

11 CONVENT AT EPHRATA, NEAR READING, PENNSYLVANIA.
Original caption: THE BROTHERS' AND SISTERS' HOUSES, 1881
Courtesy of the Philadelphia Museum
of Art: Given by John F. Braun

51 WAKEFIELD MILLS, circa 1882

41 STENTON, FROM THE SOUTHWEST, circa 1882

16 FOX CHASE INN, circa 1882

29 OLD RISING SUN INN, circa 1882

14 THE CUT LOOKING TOWARD CALEBRA,
circa 1912
Lithograph, 25¼ × 18¾ inches
Lent by Frank S. Schwarz and Son
Illustrated in Joseph Pennell's "Building of the Panama
Canal," *The Century Magazine*, August 1912. Also illus-
trated in *Sketches of the Panama Canal Made at the Isthmus
Especially for the New York Times*, New York Times, Octo-
ber 1912; and in "Joseph Pennell's Lithographs of the
Panama Canal," *Print Collector's Quaterly*, October 1912.

15 A FARM IN THE BROADS, 1895
Wash on paper, 12 × 18 inches
Brandywine River Museum. The Jane Collette Wilcox
Collection
Illustration for Anna Bowman's Dodd's "A Cruise
on the Norfolk Broads," *The Century Magazine*,
October 1895.

16 FOX CHASE INN, circa 1882
Etching, 14 × 17⅝ inches
Lent by the Free Library of Philadelphia
One of a series of etchings of "Views on the Old German-
town Road," by Joseph Pennell and Blanche Dillaye, *The
Pennsylvania Magazine of History and Biography*. Philadel-
phia: The Historical Society of Pennsylvania, 1882.

17 THE GATES OF PEDRO MIGUEL, circa 1912
Lithograph, 24¾ × 18¾ inches
Lent by Frank S. Schwarz and Son
Illustrated in Joseph Pennell's "Building of the Panama
Canal," *The Century Magazine*, August 1912. Also illus-
trated in *Sketches of the Panama Canal Made at the Isthmus
Especially for the New York Times*, New York Times, Octo-
ber 1912; and in "Joseph Pennell's Lithographs of the
Panama Canal," *Print Collector's Quaterly*, October 1912.

18 HOVETON CHURCH, 1895
Wash on paper, 12 × 18 inches
Brandywine River Museum. The Jane Collette Wilcox
Collection
Illustration for Anna Bowman Dodd's "A Cruise on the
Norfolk Broads," *The Century Magazine*, October 1895.

19 ILE BARBE FROM THE EAST, 1886
Pen and ink on paper, 8⅞ × 22½ inches
Collection of the Brandywine River Museum
Illustration for Philip Gilbert Hamerton's *The Saône,
A Summer Voyage*. Boston: Roberts Brothers, 1888

20 ILE BARBE TO THE RIGHT, 1886
Pen and ink on paper, 10¼ × 22½ inches
Collection of the Brandywine River Museum
Illustration for Philip Gilbert Hamerton's *The Saône,
A Summer Voyage*. Boston: Roberts Brothers, 1888.

21 IN A LOCK, circa 1889
Wash on paper, 8½ × 11 inches
Lent by the Print Division, The New York Public Library,
Astor, Lenox, and Tilden Foundations
Illustration for "The Stream of Pleasure," *The Century
Magazine*, August 1889. Also illustrated in Joseph and
Elizabeth Pennell's *The Stream of Pleasure*. London:
T. Fisher Unwin, 1891.

22 INTERIOR OF YORK MINSTER, circa 1880
Pen and gray ink wash, 23 × 15¼ inches
Lent by Childs Gallery, Boston and New York

23 INTERIOR, PLANTIN MUSEUM, ANTWERP,
1887–88
Pen and ink on paper, 8 × 9 inches
Lent by Childs Gallery, Boston and New York
Illustration for *The Century Magazine*, June 1888. Also
illustrated in Theodore L. DeVinne's *Christopher Plantin
and the Plantin-Moretus Museum at Antwerp*. New York:
Grolier Club, 1888.

24 MÂCON FROM THE RAILWAY BRIDGE, 1886
Pen and ink on paper, 5½ × 18 inches
Collection of the Brandywine River Museum
Illustration for Philip Gilbert Hamerton's *The Saône,
A Summer Voyage*. Boston: Roberts Brothers, 1888.

25 THE MILLS AT MEAUX, 1898
Pen and ink on paper, 5¾ × 12¾ inches
Lent by Childs Gallery, Boston and New York

26 MONTMERLE FROM THE SOUTH, 1886
Pen and ink on paper, 8⅝ × 22½ inches
Collection of the Brandywine River Museum
Illustration for Philip Gilbert Hamerton's *The Saône,
A Summer Voyage*. Boston: Roberts Brothers, 1888.

27 NOONTIME (HIGH NOON), 1884
Pen and ink on paper, 14¾ × 20 inches
Lent by Childs Gallery, Boston and New York
Illustration for Joseph and Elizabeth Robins Pennell's
*Two Pilgrims' Progress From Fair Florence to the Eternal City
of Rome*. Boston: Roberts Brothers, 1886. Also illustrated
in the Pennell's *An Italian Pilgrimage*. London: Seeley and
Company, 1887, 1889.

28 OLD AND NEW MILLS, VALENCIENNES, 1910
Etching, 9⅜ × 12½ inches
Lent by Childs Gallery, Boston and New York

29 OLD RISING SUN INN, circa 1882
Etching, 14 × 17⅝ inches
Lent by the Free Library of Philadelphia
One of a series of etchings of "Views on the Old German-
town Road," by Joseph Pennell and Blanche Dillaye, *The
Pennsylvania Magazine of History and Biography*. Philadel-
phia: The Historical Society of Pennsylvania, 1882.

30 OVANCHES—THE CROSS, 1886
Pen and ink on paper, 12½ × 15¼ inches
Collection of the Brandywine River Museum
Illustration for Philip Gilbert Hamerton's *The Saône,
A Summer Voyage*. Boston: Roberts Brothers, 1888.

31 PALACE THEATRE, 1886
Etching, 8⅞ × 6⅞ inches
Lent by Childs Gallery, Boston and New York

7 THE BRIDGE AT CHEMILLY, 1886

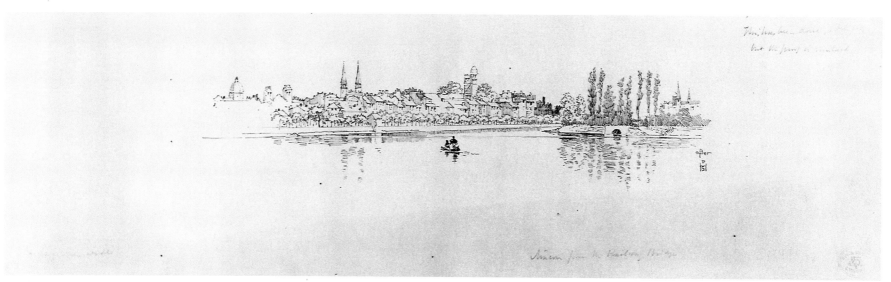

24 MÂCON FROM THE RAILWAY BRIDGE, 1886

32 THE PHILADELPHIA CLUB, THIRTEENTH AND
WALNUT STREETS, circa 1910
Lithograph, 23 × 17¾ inches
Lent by Frank S. Schwarz and Son
Illustrated in Joseph and Elizabeth Robins Pennell's
Joseph Pennell's Pictures of Philadelphia. Philadelphia:
J. B. Lippincott Company, 1914, 1926. Also illustrated in
Joseph and Elizabeth Robins Pennell's *Our Philadelphia.*
Philadelphia: J. B. Lippincott Company, 1914.

33 THE PONTE VECCHIO, FLORENCE, 1883
Etching, 9⅞ × 8 inches
Lent by Childs Gallery, Boston and New York
Illustration for *The Century Magazine,* February 1885.

34 PORTRAIT OF WASHINGTON LAKER
FROM A PHOTO BY ULKE, n.d.
Pen and ink on paper, 20 × 15 inches
Lent by the Free Library of Philadelphia

35 THE QUAY AT TREVOUX, 1886
Pen and ink on paper, 9⅜ × 22½ inches
Collection of the Brandywine River Museum
Illustration for Philip Gilbert Hamerton's *The Saône,
A Summer Voyage.* Boston: Roberts Brothers, 1888.

36 RAINY NIGHT, CHARING CROSS STATION, 1886
Etching, 7 × 8⅞ inches
Lent by Childs Gallery, Boston and New York

37 REBUILDING BROAD STREET, 1910
Lithograph, 22⅝ × 12¾ inches
Lent by Childs Gallery, Boston and New York

38 A RIVER TRAIN OR TOWED DOWN, 1886
Pen and ink on paper, 11½ × 15⅜ inches
Collection of the Brandywine River Museum
Illustration for Philip Gilbert Hamerton's *The Saône,
A Summer Voyage.* Boston: Roberts Brothers, 1888.

39 ROYAL POLYTECHNIC INSTITUTION, LONDON,
circa 1890
Pen and ink on paper, 10⅛ × 14⅛ inches
Lent by the Print Division, The New York Public Library,
Astor, Lenox, and Tilden Foundations
Illustration for "London Polytechnics and People's
Palaces," *The Century Magazine,* June 1890.

8 CASTLE ON A CLIFF IN A DISTANCE, n.d.
  Courtesy of Illustration House, Inc.

9 THE CHURCH OF SAN JUAN DE LOS REYES, TOLEDO, 1894
Courtesy of Illustration House, Inc.

46 THE SWING OF THE ARNO, PISA, 1883
  Courtesy of Childs Gallery,
  Boston and New York City

5 AT THE FOOT OF THE CROSS, 1884
Courtesy of the Glenbow Museum, Calgary, Alberta

52 THE WEST FRONT OF AMIENS CATHEDRAL, 1907
Etching, 11⅞ × 9⅞ inches
Lent by Childs Gallery, Boston and New York
Illustration for Elizabeth Robins Pennell's *French Cathedrals: Monasteries and Abbeys and Sacred Sites of France.*
New York: The Century Company, 1909.

53 Untitled Illustration, circa 1888
Wash on paper, 14 × 10 inches
Collection of Mr. and Mrs. Benjamin Eisenstat

27 NOONTIME (HIGH NOON), 1884
   Courtesy of Childs Gallery,
   Boston and New York City

Notes

[1] Joseph Pennell, *The Adventures of an Illustrator, Mostly in Following His Authors in America and Europe* (Boston: Little, Brown, 1925), p. 6.

[2] Pennell's father had previously taught at Westtown Friends Boarding School near Kennett Square in Chester County, Pennsylvania, before accepting a supervisory position with Cope Brothers, Philadelphia shipping merchants. Anne Cannon Palumbo, *Joseph Pennell and the Landscape of Change,* (Ph.D. diss., University of Maryland, 1982), p. 1.

[3] Pennell, *Adventures*, p. 9.

[4] Pennell, *Adventures*, p. 14.

[5] Pennell, *Adventures*, p. 19.

[6] Pennell, *Adventures*, pp. 24, 28, 30.

[7] Palumbo, *Pennell*, p. 16; see also Pennell, *Adventures*, p. 34.

[8] Pennell, *Adventures*, p. 43.

[9] Palumbo, *Pennell*, p. 42.

[10] Pennell, *Adventures*, pp. 65–66, 70.

[11] Elizabeth Robins Pennell, *The Life and Letters of Joseph Pennell*, 2 vols. (Boston: Little, Brown, 1929), 1:43.

[12] Pennell, *Life and Letters*, 1:44, 46–47.

[13] Pennell, *Life and Letters*, 1:86

[14] Pennell, *Life and Letters*, 1:85; Palumbo, *Pennell*, p. 124.

[15] Palumbo, *Pennell*, p. 152; Pennell, *Adventures*, p. 175.

[16] Pennell, *Life and Letters*, 1:164, 165, 166.

[17] Pennell, *Life and Letters*, 1:168, 170, 176.

[18] Frederick Keppell, "Joseph Pennell's New York Etchings at Child's Gallery," *Art Students League News* 39, no. 1 (January 1985): 1.

[19] Pennell, *Life and Letters*, 1:301.

[20] Pennell, *Life and Letters*, 1:339.

[21] Palumbo, *Pennell*, pp. 262, 260.

[22] Palumbo, *Pennell*, p. 263.

[23] Palumbo, *Pennell*, p. 284.

[24] Palumbo, *Pennell*, p. 278.

[25] Pennell, *Life and Letters*, 2:103–4.

[26] Joseph Masheck, "The Panama Canal and Some Other Works of Art," *Artforum* (May 1971): 39.

[27] Pennell, *Life and Letters*, 2:103; Palumbo, *Pennell*, p. 319.

[28] Masheck, "Panama Canal," p. 39.

[29] Palumbo, *Pennell*, p. 357.

SELECTED BIBLIOGRAPHY

Crawford, Mrs. Andrew Wright, "The Pennell Memorial Exhibition in Philadelphia," *The American Magazine of Art*, October 1926, pp. 527–528.

Elzea, Rowland. *The Golden Age of American Illustration, 1880–1914* (exhibition catalogue). Wilmington, Delaware: Delaware Art Museum, 1972.

Keppell, Frederick. "Joseph Pennell's New York Etchings at Child's Gallery," *Art Students League News*, January 1985.

Maar, Ingrid. *The Pennell Legacy: Two Centuries of Printmaking* (exhibition catalogue). Washington, D.C.: The Library of Congress, December 1983–May 1984.

Masheck, Joseph, "The Panama Canal and Some Other Works of Art," *Artforum*, May 1971, pp. 38–41.

Palumbo, Anne Cannon. *Joseph Pennell and the Landscape of Change* (Ph.D. dissertation). University of Maryland, 1982.

Pennell, Elizabeth Robins. *The Life and Letters of Joseph Pennell*, 2 vols. Boston: Little, Brown, and Company, 1929.

Pennell, Elizabeth Robins. *Our Philadelphia*. Philadelphia: J.B. Lippincott Company, 1914.

Pennell, Joseph. *The Adventures of An Illustrator*. Boston: Little, Brown, and Company, 1925.

Pennell, Joseph. *Etchers and Etchings*. New York: Macmillan Company, 1919.

Pennell, Joseph and Elizabeth Robins. *Lithography and Lithographers*. New York: Macmillan Company, 1915.

Pennell, Joseph. *Modern Illustration*. London: George Bell & Sons, 1895.

Pennell, Joseph. *Pen Drawing and Pen Draughtsmen*. New York: Macmillan Company, 1920.

Pennell, Joseph. "A Year's Experience in Practical Teaching," *The American Magazine of Art*, September 1923, pp. 469–74.

Pitz, Henry C. *Howard Pyle: Writer and Founder of the Brandywine School*. New York: Clarkson N. Porter, Inc., 1975.

Van Dyke, John C. *Memorial Exhibition of the Late Joseph Pennell, Held Under the Auspices of the Philadelphia Print Club and the Philadelphia Museum* (exhibition catalogue). Print Club of Philadelphia, October 1–31, 1926.

Weisberg, Gabriel P. and Ronnie L. Zaken. *Between Past and Present: French, English and American Etching, 1850–1950*. Cleveland: Cleveland Museum of Art, 1977.